The Coaching Allian

M000298561

Windy Dryden's pluralistic approach to coaching informs this uniquely straightforward guide to the coaching alliance. Drawing on examples from Dryden's own practice, the book explores the four specific domains of the alliance: bonds, views, objectives/goals and tasks. Dryden explains how these domains are inter-related, and how all four have an impact on the collaborative, negotiated relationship between coach and coachee.

The Coaching Alliance is a clearly written, accessible guide, with one chapter dedicated to each of the four domains. It examines each domain at different stages in the coaching process and includes key points and questions for coaches to consider in sessions with clients. By taking an alliance perspective on coaching, the coach is encouraged to think clearly and constructively about building a working relationship with their coachee, clarifying views, setting goals and completing tasks. Including a wealth of practical information, this concise book will be essential for anyone working with clients in a coaching capacity.

Windy Dryden is in part-time clinical and consultative practice and is an international authority on cognitive behavioural therapy (CBT). He is Honorary Vice President of the International Society for Coaching Psychology, was granted honorary membership in the International Association of Cognitive Behavioral Coaching in 2014 and is Emeritus Professor of Psychotherapeutic Studies at Goldsmiths University of London. He has worked in the helping professions for more than 40 years and is the author and editor of over 215 books.

Routledge Focus on Coaching

The Focus on Coaching series features books which cover an aspect of coaching particularly dear to the author's or editor's heart that they wish to share with the wider professional coaching community. The series editors are Windy Dryden and David A. Lane.

For a full list of titles in this series, please visit https://www.routledge.com/Routledge-Focus-on-Coaching/book-series/RFC

Titles in the series:

The Coaching Alliance
Theory and Guidelines for Practice
Windy Dryden

A Practical Guide to Rational Emotive Behavioural Coaching
Windy Dryden

The Coaching Alliance
Theory and Guidelines for Practice

Windy Dryden

Routledge
Taylor & Francis Group

LONDON AND NEW YORK

First published 2017 by Routledge

2 Park Square, Milton Park, Abingdon, Oxfordshire OX14 4RN
52 Vanderbilt Avenue, New York, NY 10017

Routledge is an imprint of the Taylor & Francis Group, an informa business

First issued in paperback 2019

Copyright © 2017 Windy Dryden

British Library Cataloguing-in-Publication Data
A catalogue record for this book is available from the British Library

Library of Congress Cataloging-in-Publication Data
A catalog record for this book has been requested.

ISBN: 978-1-138-08792-7 (hbk)
ISBN: 978-0-367-33905-0 (pbk)

Typeset in Times New Roman
by Apex CoVantage, LLC

Contents

1 Introduction

In this short book, I am going to discuss what I call the *coaching alliance*. In this chapter, I will begin the book by discussing the *coaching* part of the term and then the *alliance* part of the term. Finally, I will make clear the approach I am taking in this work.

1.1. Two different types of coaching

Coaching is a term that is understood differently by different people (Downey, 2014). As such, it is important that you understand what I mean by coaching, so whether you agree with my view or not, at least you will understand this view. In my opinion, there are two different types of coaching, and these types are differentiated by their different focus. These two types of coaching are (1) development-focused coaching (DF-C) and (2) problem-focused coaching (PF-C). Let me consider them one at a time.

1.1.1. Development-focused coaching (DF-C)

Let me begin by defining what I mean by development-focused coaching.

Development-Focused Coaching (DF-C) concentrates on areas of coachee development. It is rooted in an open, respectful and collaborative relationship between coach and coachee. This relationship is a fusion between what coaches bring to the process and what coachees brings to the process. DF-C's prime directive is to enable coachees, who are doing satisfactorily in life, to get more out of their life in a range of life areas. Coaches implement this directive by helping coachees (a) to set and achieve development-based objectives in one or more life domains and (b) to address the obstacles that are encountered as they pursue these objectives and their problematic responses to these obstacles. Coaches bring to the process both personal characteristics and professional expertise in the approach that informs their coaching. In utilising the latter, they will draw upon a range of strategies and techniques that are consistent with that approach and also upon strategies and techniques that stem from other coaching approaches if they are pluralistic in outlook. All interventions are carried out within a professional ethical context in which negotiated consent[1] is paramount. Coachees bring to the process a range of strengths, capabilities and resources which they will be encouraged to draw upon during the process as they strive towards reaching their development-based objectives and as they deal with obstacles along the way.

DF-C, with its emphasis on fostering the development of the coachee, is what most people think of when they hear the word coaching. You will see from this definition, however, that while the focus of coaching is on development, coachees also need to be able to help their coachees "address the obstacles that are encountered as they pursue these objectives and their problematic responses to these obstacles". When they do so, they need to be skilled in problem-focused coaching as obstacle-focused work is often synonymous with this second type of coaching.

1.1.2. Problem-focused coaching (PF-C)

Let me begin by defining problem-focused coaching.

Problem-Focused Coaching (PF-C) concentrates on coachees' practical and emotional problems of living. It, too, is rooted in an open, respectful and collaborative relationship between coach and coachee. This relationship is, again, a fusion between what coaches bring to the process and what coachees brings to the process. PF-C's prime directive is to help coachees effectively address their practical and emotional problems of living. Coaches bring to the process both personal characteristics and professional expertise in the approach that informs their coaching. In utilising the latter, they will draw upon a range of strategies and techniques that are consistent with that approach and also upon strategies and techniques that stem from other coaching approaches if they are pluralistic in outlook. All interventions are carried out within a professional ethical context in which negotiated consent[2] is paramount. Coachees bring to the process a range of strengths, capabilities and resources which they will be encouraged to draw upon during the process of addressing their problems.

While coaching was originally designed to help coachees develop themselves rather than solve problems, people also seek coaching to solve problems. As I will discuss later in the book, people with problems of living where there is a strong emotional component (henceforth called emotional problems) may prefer to seek coaching for these problems because it is more acceptable for them to do so than to seek help from a counsellor or psychotherapist. Examples of such emotional problems include anxiety about performance at work, depression about how one's career is going and anger at being criticised by one's boss. Here, you need to help your coachee deal with these emotional problems, and thus you need to have the skills to do so (see Chapter 3). I will refer to this sub-type of PF-C as *emotional problem-focused coaching* (EPF-C).

People also seek coaching for help with problems where there is not a strong emotional component (henceforth called practical problems). Examples of such practical problems include difficulties in prioritising work projects, having too much to do and feeling overwhelmed, and problems motivating one's team. Here, you need to help your coachee adopt a problem-solving approach. An example of such an approach has been provided by Palmer (2008) who has outlined a model he calls PRACTICE (where P = problem identification; R = realistic and relevant goals developed; A = alternative solutions generated; C= consideration of consequences; T = target most feasible solution; I = implementation of chosen solution; C = consolidation of the chosen potential solution; E = evaluation). I will refer to this sub-type of problem-focused coaching as *practical problem-focused coaching* (PPF-C).[3]

1.2. The coaching alliance: applying the expanded concept of the working alliance to coaching

In my view, one of the most important concepts that informs the practice of coaching is Ed Bordin's (1979) concept of the working alliance that I subsequently developed (Dryden, 2006, 2011a). Hereafter, I will refer to this as the coaching alliance.

Bordin's (1979) original paper highlighted the importance of the concept of the working alliance in the practice of psychotherapy, but he made it clear that it was also applicable to other ways of helping people. Although he did not mention coaching in his paper, it is clear that his ideas are highly pertinent to coaching. Indeed, O'Broin and Palmer (2010a: 4) have used the term *coaching alliance* and said that "the coaching alliance reflects the quality of the coachee's and coach's engagement in collaborative, purposive work within the coaching relationship, and is jointly negotiated, and renegotiated throughout the coaching process over time".

Bordin argued that the working alliance is comprised of three domains: bonds, goals and tasks. Later, I added a fourth domain, which I call "views" (Dryden, 2006). The subsequent chapters are each devoted to one domain of the coaching alliance, but I will first provide brief descriptions of these four domains (Dryden, 2012).

- *Bonds* refer to the interpersonal connectedness between the coach and coachee.
- *Views* refer to the understandings that both participants have on salient issues in coaching.
- *Goals/Objectives* refer to the purpose of the coaching meetings. In this book, I use the term *goals* when writing about the aims of PF-C and the term *objectives* when writing about the aims of DF-C.
- *Tasks* refer to the procedures carried out by both coach and coachee in the service of the latter's goals/objectives.

Please bear in mind that although I will devote one chapter to each of the domains of the coaching alliance, I see these domains as very much inter-related.

1.3. The approach taken in this book

I have written this book for all coaches, and in doing so, the approach I have taken is informed by pluralism (Cooper & McLeod, 2011). The major features of pluralism that are relevant here are as follows:

- There is no one absolute right way of conceptualising coachees' issues and objectives – different viewpoints are useful for different coachees at different points in time, and therefore, coachees need to have a broad coaching practice repertoire.
- There is no one absolute right way of practising coaching – different coachees need different things at different points in time.
- Coaches should ideally acknowledge and celebrate coachees' diversity and uniqueness.
- Coachees should ideally be involved fully at every stage of the coaching process. (O'Broin & Palmer, 2009)

My own approach to coaching is a flexible, cognitive-behavioural one that is informed by pluralism (Dryden, 2018). Although this is *not* a book on cognitive-behavioural coaching, I will, however, exemplify some of my points in the book by drawing on my own practice.

In this chapter, I have (1) outlined the pluralistic approach that I am taking in this book, (2) defined the two different types of coaching and (3) introduced the concept of the coaching alliance. Each of the following chapters is devoted to a particular domain of this alliance, beginning with the coaching bond.

2   Bonds in coaching

When considering the bond between you and your coachee, a number of issues come to the fore. In this section, I will consider the following:

- The "core conditions" of coaching
- The reflection process
- Your interactive style as coach
- The bonds of influence

2.1. The "core conditions" in coaching

If Bordin's (1979) paper is one of the most seminal in the helping literature (which includes coaching), then perhaps a paper published by Carl Rogers (1957) over 20 years earlier is perhaps the most seminal. In this article, Rogers argued that there were six conditions that were necessary and sufficient for personal change to occur. Over the years, three of these conditions have been regarded as core and have been thus called "the core conditions". These conditions are empathy, unconditional positive regard[4] and genuineness. What is important for coaches to recognise is that coachees need to experience the presence of these conditions for them to have the potency for change.

Different coaches have different views on the necessity and sufficiency of these conditions. My own view is that it is important, but not necessary, for coachees to experience their coaches as empathic, accepting[5] and genuine in their interaction. For some coaches, a particular "core condition" may be more helpful to them than others. Thus, one coachee may value your honesty more than your acceptance of them. This raises the question concerning how you can tell which condition your coachee values more than others. This question naturally leads us to a discussion of what I call the "reflection process", which is a key aspect of what it means for you and your coachee to be pluralistic partners in the coaching process.

2.2. The reflection process in coaching

I mentioned in Chapter 1 that the approach to coaching taken in this book is influenced by pluralism. As such, it adheres to a version of what has become known as George Kelly's[6] first principle. It states: "If you want to know what is wrong with someone, ask them, they may tell you" (Bannister & Fransella, 1986). The version which underpins what I call the "reflection process" in coaching is as follows: "If you want to know what is right and wrong for your coachee, ask them, they may tell you". The reflection process is interactive and not only incorporates the coachee's view, but also the coach's. What is particularly constructive is what comes out of the resultant discussion especially if you privilege your coachee's viewpoint rather than your own.

In one of the Marx Brothers' movies, Groucho stops the action and gives a reflective commentary on what has just happened. The reflection process in coaching is similar in that the coach and coachee reflect on what has transpired, is transpiring or may transpire between them. This may be done formally, for example, in a review session or by feedback at the end of a session feedback, or it may be done more informally during the process of coaching.

I used to think that this reflection process, which I see as a forum for coach and coachee to discuss matters pertaining to the coaching in which they are involved, was "extra to" or "outside" coaching. I now see it as an integral part of coaching and a vehicle for demonstrating the state of the relationship with respect to the degree of mutual respect, acceptance and trust present in that relationship.

2.3. Interactive style in coaching

The third area relevant to the coaching bond concerns the interactive style adopted by both coachee and coach and the degree of goodness of "fit" between these respective styles. Coaching alliance theory proposes that the coaching bond can be enhanced when the fit between the interactive styles of coach and coachee is good and can be threatened when such a fit is poor. Different approaches to coaching put forward preferred interactive styles between coach and coachee. For some coaches, the preferred interactive style is where the two participants are actively collaborating in using whatever approach is being taken to the coachee's issues. Such coaches like to contrast this collaborative interactive style with a more challenging style which other coaches seem to favour.

Pluralistic approaches to coaching see the coachee as an active participant in the coaching process and able to state their own preferences about which coach interactive style would most help them to achieve their coaching goals and/or objectives. This may mean adopting a challenging style with some coachees and a didactic, teaching style with others. The more coaches can authentically modify their interactive style with different coachees, the greater number of coachees they are likely to help.

Coach interactive styles may vary along a continuum rather than existing as either/or categories. The following are common style dimensions on which coaches may locate themselves according to coach variability:

*   High activity/low activity
*   Formality/informality
*   Humour/seriousness
*   Uses self-disclosure/does not use self-disclosure

Of course, I am not suggesting, for example, that once a coach has decided to use self-disclosure with a client, they not she would use it as the predominant interactive style. Rather, they would use such disclosure to make an appropriate point with that coachee when the opportunity presented itself, while she might not do so with another coachee. Contrast this with a coach who would not use self-disclosure with either coachee.

2.3.1. Issues with respect to interactive style

A full consideration of the issue of interactive style in coaching would require a volume by itself. For the present purpose, I want to make the following points.

2.3.1.1. Gauging which interactive style to adopt

It is not an easy matter to gauge which interactive style to adopt with which coachee. However, following George Kelly's suggestion that if you want to know things from coachees, it is best to ask them directly, one major way is to do just that. For example, with one of my coachees who was seeking problem-focused coaching for a problem in living (anxiety), I proceeded as follows.

Windy: Which interactive style would you advise me to adopt to enable you to get the most out of the coaching process?
Anita: That's a difficult one. I'm not sure what you mean. . . .
Windy: Well, for example, would it be more helpful to you if I adopted an active or a passive interactive style?
Anita: An active one as long as you allow me to be active as well.
Windy: That's fine. Now would you prefer me to be more informal or formal?
Anita: Definitely informal. I am not one for much formality
Windy: What about humour?
Anita: Well coaching is a serious business, but I do respond to humour when it helps me to put things into perspective.
Windy: Would it help or not if occasionally I shared something of my own experience if it shed light on how you can address the problem for which you are seeking help?
Anita: I would find that helpful if it were relevant. It would make me feel that I wasn't a freak.

From this segment, we have discovered that Anita thought that she would be helped most if I adopted an active, informal, humorous, self-disclosing style. While this was not a guaranteed recipe for success, it did provide me with some tentative guidelines for proceeding with Anita with respect to my interactive style. As with other issues, the issue of the coach's interactive style can be discussed by coach and coachee as part of the reflection process discussed earlier.

It is also possible for coaches to get such information in questionnaire form from their coachees. Thus, Lazarus (1989) used a number of questions with respect to clients' preferences concerning their therapists' interactive style in his Life History Questionnaire (LHQ). These can be modified for use in coaching as follows:

- How do you think a coach should interact with his or her coachees?
- What personal qualities do you think the ideal coach should possess?

To this I might add the following:

- Which interactive style would you advise your coach to adopt if he or she were to get the most out of you as a coachee?

• Which interactive style would you advise your coach not to adopt when working with you, and why?

2.3.1.2. Adopting a style that does not reinforce coachees' problems/issues

When two people come together in any interpersonal setting, their interactive styles may mesh or jar. Just because such styles may mesh should not necessarily be taken as a sign that effective coaching is taking place. For, what may mesh may be unproductive. While some coaches value the principle of coach–coachee collaboration, there is a danger that, in some cases, such collaboration where the coach is active may "pull" for coachee passivity. If a coachee becomes passive, this may in turn pull for greater coach activity, and a vicious cycle may be established, which may mirror and reinforce the coachee's client's passivity issues in their everyday life. Effective coaches are aware of the dangers of adopting a coaching style that reinforces their coachees' problems or issues and guard against doing this. In addition to high levels of coach activity with a passive coachee, the following are examples of coach styles that may particularly reinforce coachees' problems or issues.

2.3.1.2.1. UNDUE COACH WARMTH WITH COACHEES WHO HAVE A STRONG NEED FOR APPROVAL

Here the coachee's need for the coach's approval is gratified, but this need is reinforced to the extent that they become fearful in case their coach withdraws his or her approval (see interview with Ellis in Dryden, 1997). Here the coach needs to be less warm and to target the coachee's need for approval for change (with the coachee's agreement of course), helping them to see the negative effect that such a need may have on their life.

2.3.1.2.2. COACH DIRECTIVENESS WITH COACHEES WHO ARE HIGHLY REACTANT

A coachee who is highly reactant has an adverse reaction to actual or perceived attempts to influence them. Given this tendency, you as coach need to emphasise coachee choice more than usual. Failure to do this may lead your coachee to leave coaching as a way of preserving their autonomy.

2.3.1.2.3. COACH HUMOUR WITH COACHEES WHO USE HUMOUR AS A DEFENCE

It is well known that people can use humour as a way of defending themselves against their emotional pain and from dealing with their problems in an effective manner. If you employ humour with such a coachee, particularly in emotional problem-focused coaching (EPF-C), you unwittingly reinforce this tendency. When it helps strengthen a defence, it is often introduced by your coachee themself, and in this case, you need to respond without joining the coachee's levity. When humour is effective, it helps promote change, and this will be apparent in both PF-C and DF-C.

2.3.1.3. Coach authenticity

I have stressed the importance of the coach demonstrating interactive flexibility in coaching. However, this needs to be done genuinely, and putting on an act for a coachee may not be immediately noticed, but it will be discerned eventually with deleterious effects on the coaching alliance. Applying Lazarus's (1993) ideas to coaching, an effective coach needs to be an "authentic chameleon": in this context, being able to modify one's interactive style from patient to patient, but to do so authentically. It is part of a coach's training to become aware of his or her range of interactive styles and to be able to employ this range genuinely with different coachees at different stages of the coaching process.

2.4. The bonds of influence

In the 1980s, work emerging from social psychology in North America suggested that it was useful to consider the coaching relationship as an interpersonal setting where influence takes place (Dorn, 1984). This point of view is not very popular with coaches who tend to be uncomfortable with the notion that they influence their coachees, preferring instead to see themselves as facilitating coachee growth. However unpalatable the 'coaching as influence' idea is to some, I have found it a useful way of thinking about why coachees listen to their coaches, independent of the message that the coach is trying to convey to them.

Although I am considering here how coaches influence their coachees, it is more accurate to say that coachees allow themselves to be influenced by their coaches. They do so for three major reasons:

1) Because they like their coach or find them *attractive* in some way. I am not primarily thinking of physical attractiveness here, although this may be the case.

2) Because they find their coach *trustworthy* (Gyllensten & Palmer, 2007; O'Broin & Palmer, 2010b).
3) Because they are impressed by their coach's *credibility* as a coach. This may include the coach's expertise, experience and/or credentials. It may also be because they think the coach knows what they are talking about because they have had personal experience of the problem for which the coachee is seeking help (in PF-C) or of the objective towards which the coachee is striving (in DF-C).

Let me show you what I mean here. What mattered to one of my coachees, Anita (who we met earlier) was that I had written a number of books on anxiety (Dryden, 2000, 2003, 2011b) and was thus deemed by her to be an expert. She had already consulted two other coaches who, while competent, lacked the external trappings of expertise that Anita valued.

Taking this framework, it is possible to ask coachees the following question as part of the initial phase of coaching. "Are you most likely to listen to your coach and give credence to what they have to say, if you like the person, if you trust the person or if the person appears to know what they are talking about?" and be guided by their answer in thinking about how to best influence them. My view is that coaches should endeavour to meet their coachees' preferences on this matter to the extent that they are able to do so genuinely and to the extent that it is helpful for their coachees for them to do so.

My own experience as a coach, trainer and supervisor is that some coachees may listen to and allow themselves be influenced by coachees whom they like, but who do not show expertise, and others may listen to and allow themselves to be influenced by those who are expert, but whom they may not like. However, few coachees will listen to coachees whom they do not find trustworthy although they may like them or be impressed by their credentials.

One question that arises from this analysis is the following: to what extent should you as coach modify your approach to meet your coachee's influence preferences? Thus, if you discover that one of your coachees is most likely to listen to you if they like you, to what extent should you emphasise your likeability with this coachee? Conversely, if you discover that your coachee is most impressed by your credentials/expertise, to what extent should you emphasise these features in your coaching? These are pertinent questions to discuss with your coaching supervisor.

In an ideal world, coachees would be impressed by the content of what you say irrespective of whether they like you or whether you have demonstrable expertise. However, in the real world of coaching, how the messenger is perceived often determines the potency of the message.

Having considered the bonds of coaching in the next chapter, I will consider a domain of the alliance that I introduced (Dryden, 2006, 2011a): views.

3 Views in coaching

Effective coaching, in my opinion, is based on a number of agreed understandings between you and your coachee. Disagreement over any facet of coaching means that it is more likely that coaching will falter or fail than if agreement on these facets occurs. As such, any such disagreements need to be identified, discussed and resolved. This is only possible if you are both explicit about what you expect from yourself and from your coachee during coaching. This chapter, therefore, assumes that you will be explicit as a coach and will foster such explicitness in your coachee.

Bordin (1979), the originator of the tripartite model of the working alliance that informs much of this book did not put forward views as a separate domain of the alliance. I have found it valuable to include it as such when reflecting on my own practice as a coach and as an aid in training and supervising coaches (Dryden, 2006, 2011a).

3.1. Negotiated consent

I will begin my discussion of the views domain of the coaching alliance by focusing on the principle of negotiated consent. I have decided to use this term rather than the more usual term *informed consent*, because it reflects the greater reality of you and your coachee negotiating important parts of the contract between you. The term, "informed consent", tends to mean that your coachee is informed by you about relevant aspects of your coaching practice and, on the basis of so being informed, gives their consent to proceed with coaching on that basis. This seems to me to be a one-way process and does not allow for you, the coach, to be informed by what the coachee wants and for you to decide whether there are any elements in your coachee's preferences that you disagree with and want to negotiate about. On the basis of this discussion and negotiation, you can choose to give your consent to proceed or to withhold it just as your coachee can. The term *negotiated consent*, therefore, better reflects the pluralistic nature of coaching where the views of the coachee are taken very seriously, and they are deemed to be an equal partner in the coaching process. From the coachee's perspective, if consent cannot be negotiated, then the coachee cannot be said to consent to the process, and therefore coaching should not proceed. If it does, then this practice would not generally be regarded as ethical.

I will now turn my attention to the issues you need to cover to which your coachee after discussion and negotiation should be asked to give their consent. These are

- the nature of coaching;
- the nature of the specific approach to coaching that you practise;
- the roles and responsibilities of all interested parties;
- confidentiality and its limits; and
- the practicalities of coaching.

Based on Garvin and Seabury's (1997) work, I make a distinction between an *enquirer*, an *applicant* and a *coachee*. When a person is in the enquiring role, they think they want coaching and are shopping around to see if they can make a decision about whether or not to seek coaching in a formal sense, and if so, how to find a suitable coach. When the person is in the applicant role, they have decided to seek coaching and have decided to have you as their coach. At this point you need to discuss and negotiate a number of issues with them, at the end of which period if they give their consent to go forward, they become your coachee, as long as you give your consent too.

3.1.1. The nature of coaching

It is important that you and the person seeking coaching help from you are in agreement about the nature of coaching and that coaching is best suited for what the coachee is seeking. In this book, as I have said, I am considering two forms of coaching: development-focused coaching and problem-focused coaching. In the first, coaching is for people who are doing OK in life, but want more. They are looking to get more from themselves, from their work, from their relationships and from their lives. In the second, coaching is for people seeking help for practical and emotional problems in living. While coaching evolved to help coachees further their development, practically it transpired that some people also sought coaching for help with problems in living. They did this because it was more acceptable for them to seek help from a coach than from a counsellor or therapist. Seeking help from the latter can conjure up the idea that there is something wrong with them that needs fixing, an idea that, rightly or wrongly, puts them off seeking help from a counsellor or therapist. Seeking help from a coach, by contrast, has less negative connotations for such people. Consulting a coach does not mean that there is anything wrong with them; it means that they are an ordinary person with a common problem. Coaches were thus being asked to help people who, before the advent of coaching, sought help from counsellors or therapists for their problem, albeit in some cases reluctantly, for reasons given above. In many cases, this meant that coaches were being asked to help people who had emotional problems with which they, the coaches, were not equipped to deal. This was particularly the case with coaches who had no prior training in counselling and psychotherapy. For those who did, it was far less of a problem. Indeed, it is my view that coaches who have had training and experience both in counselling/psychotherapy and in coaching are well equipped to work in development-focused coaching and emotional problem-focused coaching. In training coaches, my aim is to equip them to work in both DF-C and PF-C (particularly EPF-C). However, when it comes to the latter, if they have not had prior training in counselling or psychotherapy, they need to understand for which problems EPF-C is suited and for which problems it is not. With applicants seeking coaching for their emotional problems, it is also important that they understand the indications and contra-indications for EPF-C. Before I consider this issue, I want to make it clear that this discussion with applicants can happen before you outline the specific nature of the specific approach to coaching that you take or afterwards. At what point you have this discussion is determined more by applicant variability than by any rules of procedure.

3.1.1.1. *When coaches have emotional problems: the indications and contraindication for emotional problem-focused coaching (EPF-C)*

Cavanagh (2005), in an important chapter on mental health issues in executive coaching, outlined a number of guidelines to help coaches decide whether or not to offer coaching to executives in distress. I have used his guidelines to help coaches to decide whether or not to offer applicants EPF-C for their emotional problems. I am writing this for those coaches who have been trained in both forms of coaching, but who do not have formal professional training in counselling/psychotherapy. Unless there is a good reason not to, I suggest that you make the following points clear to an applicant so that you can have an open discussion on this issue.

1   *How long has the applicant been experiencing the emotional problem?*

If the emotional problem is of recent origin or if it occurs intermittently, then EPF-C may be considered. However, if it occurs persistently or is chronic, then EPF-C is not indicated, and a judicious referral to a mental health specialist may be required.[7]

2   *How extreme are the responses of the applicant?*

If the applicant's emotional, behavioural and/or thinking responses to the relevant adversity are distressing to the person, but lie within a mild to moderate range of distress, then EPF-C may be considered. However, if the applicant's distress is extreme, then EPF-C is not indicated.

3   *How pervasive is the emotional problem?*

If the applicant's emotional problem is limited to a certain situation or aspect of the person's life, then EPF-C may be considered. However, if it occurs in many situations and on many occasions, then EPF-C is not indicated.

4   *How defensive is the applicant with respect to their emotional problem?*

The applicant may meet the above three criteria with respect to the emotional problem for which they are seeking help, but still not be suitable for EPF-C because of their high level of defensiveness with respect to the problem. Signs of this include: (a) actively seeking to avoid addressing the problem; (b) being told that they have to seek help by someone and denying they have the problem themselves; (c) showing in their responses that they would struggle to cooperate with the coach when addressing the problem.

5   *How resistant to change is the emotional problem?*

If it appears that the emotional problem is likely to persist despite the applicant's apparent willingness to address it, then this may indicate that the applicant is likely to have great difficulty in addressing the problem. While this can only really be judged once you and the applicant have decided to work together to address the problem in EPF-C (and when this occurs, the applicant has become a coachee), if the person has failed to address the problem several times before in different ways, then this may be a contraindication for EPF-C. My advice here would be this. If the applicant's emotional problem is intermittent, non-pervasive, non-extreme and if the applicant indicates they can cooperate with you, then if their problem has seemed resistant to change in the past, offer to take them on if you can offer a fresh approach to the problem and one that makes sense to them, and that they will agree to be referred to someone with more experience at dealing with the emotional problem than you if the problem continues to be resistant to change.

3.1.1.2. Examples of problems dealt with in PF-C

Here are examples of coachee's problems in living (both practical and emotional) that coaches have indicated in their promotional material that they have dealt with in PF-C. They can thus be seen as indicators for PF-C (assuming that the above five criteria are also met). Thus, in a work context, one coaching website[8] lists the following issues for which they claim their coachees have sought help and successfully dealt with using coaching:

- Managing challenging situations with colleagues/bosses/clients
- Managing underperformance
- Managing excessive workload/managing stress
- Dealing with fear of failure (and success)
- Managing conflicting demands of work and personal life
- Fear of public speaking/giving presentations
- Desire to be more assertive/improve personal impact
- Coping with redundancy

In a personal coaching context, another website[9] says that coaching (or what I am calling here problem-focused coaching or PF-C) seeks to help coachees to

- Become more assertive with friends and family;
- Tackle people and situations that they have avoided;
- Overcome a personal block such as taking up a healthier lifestyle. Other blocks might include stress, confidence issues, overcoming negative thinking, perfectionism and dealing with work related difficulties.

3.1.2. *The nature of the specific approach to coaching that you practise*

Once you and the person have agreed that either development-focused coaching or problem-focused coaching is suitable for the person, and you both want to proceed on that basis, you then need to explain the nature of the specific approach to coaching that you take so that the person applying for help can make a decision to proceed or not. This does not mean that you will give the person a lecture on the approach. What it means is that you will give the person some indication about what your approach to DF-C or PF-C is likely to entail for them and what they can reasonably expect from you.[10]

3.1.2.1. *The nature of your specific approach to development-focused coaching*

When you outline the nature of your specific approach to DF-C, I suggest that you stress that your main role is initially to help the person to select areas of their life in which they wish to develop themself and to explain what your approach says about the factors that need to be considered when this is done. Thus, an existential coach may have different concepts in mind to a cognitive-behavioural coach. Usually, you will help them to construct an action plan which will then guide the behaviours that they need to take to achieve their objective. Your main task, here, is to help them to adjust their behaviours on the basis of their experiences in implementing the plan. How you do this will depend on your approach, and this should be made clear. If the person encounters an obstacle along the way and experiences a set of problematic responses to that obstacle, then you need to help them understand the factors involved and then deal with them. Once again, what these factors are will be guided by your specific approach. In helping the person deal with their problematic responses to the encountered obstacle you have moved from practising DF-C to EPF-C, and your coaching contract needs renegotiating accordingly.

It is also important to point out to the person seeking your help that although you have a perspective on what they discuss with you and that this perspective is informed by whatever approach you practise, you are also flexible and pluralistic in approach and will seek and incorporate the person's own perspective when agreeing a shared view on their objectives and on which concepts these objectives should be based.

3.1.2.2. The nature of your specific approach to problem-focused coaching

When you outline the nature of your approach to PF-C, I suggest that you stress that your main role is to encourage the person seeking help to specify and focus on their problem. You will offer them an understanding of the problem and how the person is unwittingly maintaining it, based on the relevant factors that seem to underpin the problem and that are emphasised in your specific approach to PF-C. However, again it is important that you make clear that you are flexible and pluralistic in your practice of PF-C and that you will seek and incorporate the person's own perspective on these matters when agreeing a shared view of their problem and what they need to do to deal with it effectively.

My own approach to PF-C (especially EPF-C) is based on the work of Albert Ellis (Katsikis, Kostogiannis, & Dryden, 2016). Here is how I outlined the nature of my approach to EPF-C for a person seeking coaching for an emotional problem in living.

In this case, please note that I knew that the person's problem was an emotional problem rather than a practical one, and I incorporated this into my explanation. If I knew nothing about the person's problem, my explanation would have been more general and would have included both emotional problem-solving and practical problem-solving.

> *There are a number of approaches to coaching for problems, and it is important that you understand something of the one that I practise, which is known as Cognitive-Behavioural Coaching (CBC). This approach is based on the idea that the way a person thinks, feels and acts has a very important role to play in a person's problem. My own approach to CBC focuses a lot on the attitudes that a person holds towards the adversity that re-occurs in their problem and the way they act when their attitude comes to the fore. As a practitioner of CBC, I will help you to identify, examine and change the attitudes that seem to be underpinning the problem and help you to develop more not for helpful attitudes. I will also help you to act in ways that are consistent with these more helpful attitudes and that will help you to strengthen these attitudes.*

If your outline of your specific approach to PF-C makes sense to the person, you may proceed to discussing the roles and responsibilities of all stakeholders in the person's coaching. If it does not make sense to the person, try and find out with which approach to problem-based coaching they may better resonate and effect a referral to a practitioner of that approach.

3.1.3.   The roles and responsibilities of all stakeholders

In life coaching, where a person seeks help from you as a coach in independent practice which may include work and non-work issues, then the two of you are the main stakeholders in the work (Grant & Cavanagh, 2010). This is the case particularly when the person is responsible for paying for their own coaching. When the person is being funded by someone else (e.g. their employing organisation), this generally means that this someone else has a stake in the person's coaching (and are thus a stakeholder) and also has roles and responsibilities that need to be made clear.

Let me begin with the more straightforward situation where you and the person in the applicant role need to be clear and agree with one another with respect to your respective roles and responsibilities.

3.1.3.1. Your role as a coach

In my view, you need to be clear about the following with respect to your role as a coach:

- In DF-C, your role is to help the person to identify life areas that they wish to discuss with the purpose of setting developmental-based objectives in each of these areas. Then you will help them to plan to achieve these objectives and deal with any obstacles that occur along the way and with any problematic responses to these obstacles that your coachee experiences. You will need to agree an endpoint to coaching, but this may change as coaching unfolds.
- In PF-C, your role is to help the person identify and understand the problem for which they are seeking help and encourage them to set a goal with respect to this problem. Then, you need to help the person plan to change the factors that explain the problem (illuminated by your specific approach to PF-C) and again help them deal with any obstacles that occur and with problematic responses to these obstacles. As in DF-C, you will need to agree an endpoint to PF-C, but it is important to enquire whether the person may want to transfer to a DF-C contract once they have reached their goal.

3.1.3.2. Your responsibilities as a coach

In my view, you need to be clear about the following with respect to your responsibilities as a coach:

- In both forms of coaching, you have the responsibility to safeguard the welfare of your coachee and that of anybody to whom they pose a risk. In such cases, you may have to break the coach–coachee confidential relationship (see later), and thus, the person needs to understand this and agree to it before you accept them as a coachee.
- In DF-C, you need to inform the person what are the limits of your expertise. Thus, some DF coaches have not had any prior training in counselling/psychotherapy and thus would not have the necessary skills to help coachees who experience a problematic response to any obstacles that they encounter on the road to achieving their DF-C objectives. It is important to inform applicants for DF-C that you will refer them to someone who does have the skills to help them if this occurs.
- In PF-C, you also have to inform the person of the limits your expertise. While you may have been trained to deal with non-clinical emotional problems of living, you may not have been trained to deal with problems that are more clinical in nature.[11] It is again important to inform applicants for PF-C (and mainly EPF-C) that you will refer them to someone who does have the skills to help them if this occurs.

3.1.3.3. Your coachee's role

All coaching approaches work better when coachees are active in the process (Ianiro, Lehmann-Willenbrock, & Kauffeld, 2015). This means that your coachee needs to understand that they need to take an active role in coaching in a number of ways including

- Being as clear as they can be about what they want from the coaching process
- Negotiating with you about the best way to solve their problem(s) or to achieve their coaching objective(s)
- Committing to put into practice any "homework" tasks that they have negotiated with you to take forward the coaching process
- Being honest in giving you feedback about what is helpful and unhelpful about coaching

•   Being clear about obstacles encountered during the coaching process
     and engaging with you in understanding and dealing with them

3.1.3.4. Your coachee's responsibilities

At the outset, it is important that you ask the person if there is anything that
you should know about them that might negatively impact the coaching
process or make it unviable, and it is the person's responsibility to be honest
about this. Such information may include the time the person has or is willing to devote to coaching and any pre-existing physical or psychological
issues (e.g. addiction) that they have which may limit the effectiveness of
coaching. One of my coachees did not disclose at the outset that he smoked
marijuana every day, which eventually explained his lack of active partici-
pation in the coaching process.

3.1.3.5. The roles and responsibilities of stakeholders

As I mentioned above, a stakeholder is a third party who has a stake in
your coachee's coaching. This is usually, but not exclusively, the person's
employer who is funding their coaching. The role of a stakeholder is to be
supportive of the coachee's efforts, and here it is important for the stakeholder to make clear what they are and what they are not prepared to do to
help the coachee. Thus, some employers will make clear *when* they will
allow coachees to make appointments with you and *when not*. While others will state that if a conflicting meeting is scheduled at a time when you
and your coachee have agreed to meet, their employee (i.e. your coachee)
is expected to attend that meeting. Once this is made clear, you and your
coachee need to discuss whether or not you are both prepared to consent to
this. Some coaches will not consent to this situation while others will do so,
as long as their cancellation policy is respected (see below).

The stakeholder also needs to make clear if they have objectives or goals
for the coachee and if so, what they are. A common scenario is when an
employer refers a person for coaching for their "anger problem" and wants
to see improvement in this area as a result of "anger management coaching". Quite often the person referred does not agree with the stakeholder's
view, and this needs to be fully discussed before consent from you and your
coachee can be given. Some stakeholders are willing to be a part of the
negotiation, if invited by you and your coachee, but others are not willing
to do this.

If you work regularly with a stakeholder, you will have an opportunity to form an alliance with them and make clear what your position is on some of these issues. Please remember that stakeholders may have some misconceptions about coaching and may benefit from your education on such points.

3.1.4. Confidentiality and its limits

Like other forms of helping, coaching cannot be completely confidential, and as such, you need to state clearly and, preferably in writing, what are the exceptions to complete confidentiality. These exceptions are likely to be legal in that you will likely break confidentiality to protect the life or well-being of your coachee – if the latter is not prepared to protect their own interests in this respect – and to protect the life and well-being of those to whom your coachee poses a risk. In addition, disclosures of past child abuse or sex with a minor do have to be reported to the authorities and you are obliged to disclose notes if required to do so by the courts or if your coachee provides legal mandate for their disclosure.

In cases where your coachee's coaching is funded by a third party (e.g. the person's employer), the question may arise concerning what to disclose if anything to that third person. Some coaches have a blanket policy that they will not disclose any information about their coachees to the latter's employers (or other third party), and if this is your position, then you need to be make this to your coachee and to their employer (in the latter case, this should form part of your contract with them). Other coaches are prepared to disclose information in the form of a progress report to the third party, but only in a form that is acceptable to the coachee. From a coaching alliance perspective, your position should be made clear to the coachee who can then give their consent to proceed with coaching (or not) based on a negotiation of any points they want to put forward for consideration by you. For more information about the ethics of coaching see Iordanou, Hawley, and Iordanou (2017).

3.1.5. The practicalities of coaching

The fifth area of coaching that you need to be clear about at the outset concerns what might be called the practicalities of coaching. From a coaching alliance perspective, what is important here is that both you and your coach are clear concerning what to expect from one another in each of the following areas.

3.1.5.1. The length and frequency of coaching sessions and the duration of coaching

These matters can either be fixed at the outset of coaching or they can vary as the coaching process unfolds. For example, the frequency of coaching is quite likely to change with sessions becoming spaced out as your coachee makes progress towards problem solution or objective achievement. I find it useful to have a clear starting off point on these matters, but to agree that these can be renegotiated as coaching proceeds. Some coaches prefer to offer 50-minute sessions, but others offer 90-minute sessions, and this needs to be agreed at the outset. Some coachees find very long sessions draining, while for others the intensity is useful.

3.1.5.2. The medium of coaching

Coaching can occur in a variety of media (e.g. non-virtual face-to-face, Skype or similar platform or telephone). Virtual coaching is appealing to a lot of coaches and coachees. For the former, Skype sessions can be conducted at home, thus saving on the expense of hiring an office. For the latter, it allows virtual face-to-face contact while saving on the time it takes for the coachee to get to the coach's office. My own view is that there is something more engaging about face-to-face coaching, particularly at the beginning of the process, but as the coaching relationship develops and the coachee makes progress then virtual coaching, with its time-saving benefits, it can be very useful. Again, it is important to have a clear agreement on how coaching will proceed, but you need to recognise that some coachees do not want to be coached by Skype or telephone. The benefits of virtual coaching have been summarised by Clutterbuck (2010).

3.1.5.3. Your fee, how it is to be paid and who is responsible for paying it

It is important that your coachee is clear what your fee is, particularly if they are paying for their coaching themself. However, in my view, it is important that they know what you are charging their employer if the latter is paying you directly. This enables all stakeholders to have the same information, as there is something disenfranchising when the coachee is in the dark about an important aspect of coaching. However, if the coachee does not wish to know how much their employer is paying you, then they have a right not to know.

My own practice concerning when to be paid is probably influenced by my prior training in counselling and psychotherapy in that in these helping professions the client pays after a session is taken place. I am personally uncomfortable about being paid before I have rendered a service. However, receiving payment in advance is quite common in coaching, and sometimes coaches want their coachees or the coachees' sponsors to pay for the entire amount of coaching upfront. Again, from a coaching alliance perspective, the important point is that all parties agree on this issue.

3.1.5.4. Your cancellation policy

It is important that you are clear concerning the nature of your cancellation policy, and the best way of doing so is in writing to avoid possible misunderstandings later. Many coaches state that they have a 24-hour cancellation policy. My own practice as a coach is to require a 48-hour notice of cancellation, and I am very clear in what I write that this is different from giving two-day notice. If 48-hour notice is not given, then I will charge for the session. The exceptions to this are if the coachee or members of their family require unforeseen emergency hospital treatment. Thus, I will charge if the required notice is not given and the coachee cannot attend a session because, for example, they have developed influenza, need to attend an urgent business meeting, cannot travel because of a transportation strike or go to collect a child from school who has been taken ill, but does not require emergency hospital treatment.

Having said this, I demonstrate parity in the coaching relationship by informing coachees that they will get a free coaching session if I cancel a session and have not given the coachee 48-hour notice of cancellation – unless I, or one of my immediate family, require unforeseen emergency hospital treatment.

3.1.5.5. Coach–coachee contact

In some forms of psychotherapy, the therapist discourages the client from making any contact between sessions, save in an emergency or to change an appointment. Coaching tends to be less prescriptive on this issue although I know that some coaches tend to get irritated with their coachees who make frequent between-session contacts. Thus, it is important that you negotiate an agreement between you and your coachee concerning contact between sessions that suits you both. If between-session contact occurs, then the issue of payment for such contact needs to be addressed, and this can become complicated. For this reason, some coaches quote a total price for coaching that includes a set number of full sessions and a set number of between-session contacts. As before, the important issue is not what is agreed, but that an agreement has been made by you and your coachee to which you both commit.

In summary, negotiated consent involves your coachee giving consent once they have heard your position on a number of issues, having given their position on these issues and negotiated a position to which you both can consent.

3.1.6. Views on coachee problems and obstacles

From the perspective of the coaching alliance, it is very important that you and your coachee agree on what problem(s) you are both going to address in PF-C and what obstacles you are both going to tackle in both forms of coaching.[12]

3.1.6.1. Selecting a target problem

First, you both need to be clear whether or not the problem for which your coachee is seeking help is one that is appropriate for coaching rather than therapy/counselling (see pp. 17–19). Then, if your coachee has several problems that they wish to address in coaching, it is important that you select which problem you are going to start with. I call this the "target problem" since you and your coachee are targeting the problem for change. While it is usual for you to go along with your coachee's selection on this issue, occasionally, you may think that it might be better to start with a different problem. Here, it is important that you voice your opinion and provide reasons for this. Then, you can discuss this issue openly with your coachee. The important point here and elsewhere from a coaching alliance perspective is that you and your coachee agree on which problem you are going to address and, later, that you keep to this focus unless there is a good and agreed reason to change focus.

3.1.6.2. Selecting a target obstacle

Coaching, like the course of true love, rarely runs smoothly, and your coachee is likely to encounter a number of potential obstacles in the form of adversities, both in DF-C – as they work towards their development-based objective, and in PF-C – as they work words their problem-based goal.

I make the following distinction between a potential obstacle and an actual obstacle in this book.[13] A potential obstacle is something that your coachee anticipates that might derail their coaching work, but has not yet occurred. You can discuss what productive steps your coachee might take to prevent the obstacle from occurring. An actual obstacle is something that has occurred and has derailed the coaching work. Your coachee may or may not have a disturbed response to the obstacle. When they do not have a disturbed response, the obstacle is regarded as a practical problem and can be dealt with using PPF-C. When they do have a disturbed reaction, this is regarded as an emotional problem and can be dealt with using EPF-C.

Obstacles may be directly related to the work that your coachee is doing with you in either form of coaching, or they may be unrelated to such work. An example of the latter would be the sudden illness of a loved one which is completely unrelated to the work your coachee is doing with you in coaching.

Sometimes, your coachee may have not make two or more disturbed responses to the same negative event. For example, Joan was working towards her development-focused coaching objective when one of her colleagues made a formal complaint against her at work. She felt shame, anxiety and anger in response to this adversity, all of which derailed the work she was doing in coaching, and thus she had three obstacles to deal with. When this happens, your job is to help your coachee to deal with these responses one at a time and, from a coaching alliance perspective, it is important that you agree on which obstacle to focus first. When you agree on one, it becomes the target obstacle. After you have dealt with this obstacle, you do the same with the second obstacle and so on if there are several to deal with as was the case with Joan.

At other times, your coachee may have not make a disturbed response to two separate, but co-occurring negative events – and thus can be said to be facing two obstacles. Again, these obstacles may or may not be directly related to the coaching work they are doing with you. Once more, from a coaching alliance perspective, the main point is that you and your coachee agree that they are both obstacles and agree on the order in which you are both going to address them.

3.1.6.3. Understanding a target problem or obstacle[14]

Another important aspect of the views domain of the coaching alliance is that you and your coachee agree on the nature of the problem or obstacle, and this will be influenced by the constructs embedded in your specific approach to coaching.

I pointed out above that it is important for you to outline your specific coaching approach before coaching begins to help the applicant decide from their viewpoint whether or not they wish to proceed with your approach to coaching. However, it is also important for you to get the applicant's view on their own perspective on matters to do with problems and coaching. You can then develop a shared view of the problem (or obstacle)

3.1.7. Views on the coaching approach to be taken with your coachee

Earlier in this chapter, I mentioned that it is important for you to explain your specific approach to coaching to the person seeking coaching from you so that the two of you can discuss whether or not coaching along the lines of that specific approach is what the person is looking for and whether or not it is suitable to them. Such a discussion is informed by the person's own ideas about the kind of coaching they are looking for. If an agreement can be reached, negotiated consent is given by both parties to proceed. This agreement on the type of coaching to be offered to the person is done at a *general* level.

However, when you have discovered what the coachee is looking for either with respect to their development-based objectives or their problem-based goals, you are in a position to outline, in more *specific* terms, the coaching approach that you propose to take. From a pluralistic perspective, it is important that you elicit your coachee's ideas of what coaching approach they are looking for and then negotiate a way forward based on your respective inputs.

In the next chapter, I will discuss the raison d'etre of coaching: its purpose.

4 Objectives/goals in coaching[15]

People seek coaching because they want to achieve things. They may be clear about what they want to get out of coaching, or they may have a sense that they are not getting the most out of themselves at work, in their personal life or in general, but are not clear about what would make a difference to them in these respects. If they seek coaching for a problem, they may just want the problem and any pain associated with the problem to end or they may have a clear idea about what they want to achieve with respect to the problem which may or may not be achievable.

Your task in the objectives/goals domain of the coaching alliance is to agree with your coachee to set objectives (in DF-C) and goals (in PF-C) that are achievable so that you can work as a team to help the coachee achieve them.

4.1. Agreeing development-based objectives in coaching

The main task that you have in the objective alliance domain of development-focused coaching (DF-C) is to help your coachee set as many development-based objectives as they want in a variety of life areas, but you both need to be mindful of how many sessions you have contracted for. In a book that I wrote on very brief cognitive-behavioural coaching, which lasts between one and three sessions (Dryden, 2017), I argued that these time constraints mean that the VBCB coach and their coachee only have time to set and work on one development-based objective. If you have an open-ended ongoing coaching contract with your coachee, then the main thing is agreeing with them which objective you are going to choose to work on first (i.e. the target objective). While many coachees, who for one reason or another have negotiated a coaching contract based on a fixed number of sessions, are quite happy to see how the coaching process unfolds with respect to how many of their objectives they can tackle, others prefer to be clear on this issue when discussing what they want to gain from coaching. In this latter case, you and your coachee need to think about such questions as

- How many sessions you are going to have with one another?
- How many development-based objectives has your coachee set?
- In which order does your coachee wish to place their objectives?
- How many sessions are you going to devote to each objective? This may be difficult to judge, but a rough estimate is useful.
- Is there a link between the different objectives so that learning derived from pursuing one objective may be transferred to the pursuit of the other objective(s)? This may be apparent at the outset, or it will only be clear once coaching on the pursuit of objectives is underway.

4.1.1.   Development-based objectives: achievement, maintenance and enhancement

As the name suggests, a development-based objective is one that involves your coachee developing themself in some way. Development, by its nature, involves a process with no easily discernable endpoint. For example, Abraham Maslow (1968), amongst others, wrote about self-actualisation, a drive that people have to fulfil their potential. However, he saw this as an ongoing process with no endpoint. Such an endpoint would imply that it would not be possible for a person to develop himself or herself further. This is a ludicrous idea as demonstrated by Marilyn Fielding's well-known saying: "No one ever has it 'all together'. That's like trying to eat once and for all". So, when you discuss setting a development-based objective with your coachee, it is important that you do not convey the idea that the achievement of the objective is the end of the story. It may be the end of the first chapter, but there are other chapters to consider and talk about.

4.1.1.1.   Maintaining an objective that has been achieved

As anybody who has set a weight-loss target and has succeeded in reaching it will tell you, it is one thing to lose weight, and it is quite another thing to maintain the targeted new weight. As discussed above, most development-based objectives in DF-C are those that your coachee would want to maintain once achieved. For example, if your coachee wants to improve their communication skills as their development-based objective, they will probably wish to maintain these gains. Consequently, it is important that you discuss this issue fully with your coachee and then help them to select a development-based objective they can not only achieve, but also maintain.

4.1.1.2. Enhancing an objective that has been achieved

As I will discuss in the next section, one of the points you need to consider when you negotiate a development-based objective with your coachee is how they will know when they have achieved it. In addition to the issue of objective maintenance (discussed above), you and your coachee need to consider the issue of objective enhancement. For example, let's suppose again that your coachee sets "an improvement in communication skills" as their development-based objective. In some approaches to coaching, an important coachee task here is to be clear about how they would know when they have achieved this objective. In other approaches, a more general "felt sense" of achievement would be sought without concrete specification. Whichever approach is taken, your coachee's next task is to maintain these gains. Their third task, the focus of this section, concerns what would constitute enhancement of these gains. Again, in some coaching approaches, specific referents would be sought (and the coachee would be asked how would they know if they were succeeding in improving their communication skills?), while in other approaches, a more intuitive marker would be acceptable.

Another issue, and one which is important from a coaching alliance perspective, has to do with the agreement that you and your coachee need to make concerning when to switch your focus from one development-based objective to another. This is usually done when the coachee considers that they have a plan in place to enhance these skills and that they can implement this plan on their own.

4.1.2. Maximising the chances that your coachee will achieve their development-based objectives

When discussing your coachee's objectives with them, it is useful to have in mind a number of points that will inform the selection of these objectives. These are the foundations that maximise the chances that your coachee will persist in their development-related work. I will discuss points here.

4.1.2.1. Objective clarity

As noted above, some approaches to coaching hold that the clearer your coachee can be about what they want to achieve, the more likely they are to achieve it and/or to maintain it once achieved. By their nature, development-based objectives tend to be quite broad (e.g. "to become a better conflict manager", "to develop greater resilience" or "to increase my friendship circle"), and thus, it is very important that you help your coachees to be clear with themself and with you about how they and you will know when they have achieved their objective. Again, different approaches to coaching vary according to how specific or general they think these objectives ought to be. Your coachee's views on this issue are very important, and from a coaching alliance standpoint, what is also important is that you and your coachee agree on the level of specificity to be aimed for here.

4.1.2.2. Whose development-based objective is it?

Coaching is more effective if the development-based objective that your coachee has set is truly what they want to achieve. I call this objective an "intrinsic objective". Sometimes it happens that a stakeholder (often an employer) refers someone for coaching because they want the person to achieve something (e.g. improvement in communication skills). I call this objective an "extrinsic objective". When the person shares the employer's objective, that is when there is concordance between the intrinsic objective and the extrinsic objective, there is no problem. Indeed, this is a favourable situation because the employer can support the coachee's work towards their shared objective. However, when the coachee does not agree with their employer, but feels compelled to attend coaching, then there is a potential threat to the coaching alliance that you need to deal with (see below). Remember that, from a coaching alliance perspective, effective coaching occurs when you and your coachee agree on the coachee's intrinsic objective. Indeed, Gessnitzer and Kauffeld (2015) found that coaching was more effective when a coach and their coachee agreed on goals that were initiated by the latter than when they were initiated by the former. When the coach agrees with a coachee initiated objective, then the objective is much more likely to be an intrinsic objective than when the coachee agrees with a coach- or third-party-initiated objective.

4.1.2.2.1. WHEN A PERSON DISAGREES WITH A STAKEHOLDER'S OBJECTIVE
AND HAS NO INTRINSIC DEVELOPMENT-BASED OBJECTIVE

When a stakeholder (in this case an employer) refers a person for coaching, but the person does not agree with the extrinsic objective of the employer, then it is important for the coach to discover whether or not the person has an intrinsic objective for the coaching process. If not, then the person is not initially a good candidate for coaching, and you, as coach, have a number of options:

a) Do not offer the person a coaching contract and explain to the employer why. In my view, this should only happen if (1) the person gives their consent for you to do this and participates in the formulation of the communication to the employer, and (2) you have a good relationship with the employer.

b) Do not offer the person a coaching contract, but leave the person to explain the reasons to their employer.

c) Invite the person to consider the perspective of the employer before making a decision whether to follow the suggestion of the employer and target the latter's objective.

d) Invite the employer (in this case) to a three-way meeting between you, the person referred for coaching and the employer, the purpose of which is to facilitate a discussion between the referrer and the employee to determine whether or not the two can agree on the issue. If not, then in my view, you should not offer the person a coaching contract that they do not want.

4.1.2.2.2. WHEN A PERSON DISAGREES WITH A STAKEHOLDER'S OBJECTIVE, BUT DOES HAVE AN INTRINSIC DEVELOPMENT-BASED OBJECTIVE

When this is the situation then you again have a number of options.

a) Go along with the person's intrinsic development-based objective and disregard the stakeholder's objective. This shows the person that they can trust you and that you are on their side, but it may compromise your relationship with the stakeholder. In this context, Machin (2010) found that trust was particularly important in relationships between coachees and in-house coaches who, in this context, are generally employed by the stakeholder.

b) Again, with the person's permission, invite the employer (in this case) to a three-way meeting between you, the person referred for coaching and the employer, the purpose of which is to facilitate a discussion between the referrer and the employee to determine whether or not the two can agree on the issue. If so, offer a coaching contract; if not, proceed as with (a) above.

c)   Leave the person to resolve the issue with the employer and to return if this is done to initiate DF-C.

Two important points should be remembered here:

1   You need to agree an intrinsic development-based objective with your coachee and one that is initiated by the coachee.
2   Be mindful of the objectives of any stakeholders and involve them in the objective-setting process, if possible, and with the consent of your coachee. The purpose of this involvement is to develop a strong three-way coaching alliance if this can be done. If not, the next best thing is developing a strong two-way alliance between you and your coachee where you both have to manage the fact that your coachee may not have the stakeholder's support.

4.1.2.3. The relationship between the objective and values/ meaning

Coachees will choose development-based objectives for a variety of reasons, and quite often, they may have several reasons for selecting a single objective. It is useful to find out what these reasons are. Let's take Philip and Stuart who are both seeking coaching to improve their communication skills at work. Philip wants to do so because he values and finds meaning in having good relationships at work, while Stuart sees doing so as improving his prospects for promotion because he wants an increased salary to improve his purchasing power in life. Thus, while Philip's objective is clearly based on a value, Stuart's objective is more pragmatic.

There is nothing wrong with having a pragmatic reason for setting development-based objectives in coaching. However, in my view, when your coachee's development-based objective is based on a core value/meaning rather than pragmatic considerations, then they are more likely to persist at pursuing this objective than when such values/meaning are not present, especially when the going gets tough for them. This is particularly the case when they keep the value-objective link at the forefront of their mind. I see a value as a judgement of what is important or meaningful in life or gives purpose to that life. Although not strictly synonymous with the concept of values, I use terms like *meaning, importance* or *purpose*, if coachees don't resonate with the term *value*.

4.1.2.4. The presence or absence of social support

For coachees who are autonomous in personality structure – meaning they are self-directed and do not look towards others to support their endeavours – the presence or absence of social support is not an important issue. Indeed, the presence of social support might be a hindrance to them. However, for many of your coachees, the presence of social support is an important positive influence on them and helps them to persist at striving towards their development-based objective, particularly if the going gets tough. So, find out from your coachee if having a social support system would encourage them to pursue their objective, and if so, help them to specify who would be in this system and suggest they ask these people if they would show their support to your coachee during DF-C.

4.1.2.5. Can the objective be integrated into your coachee's life once achieved?

A year ago, I decided to increase my exercise regime. I had been doing a brisk walk six days a week, and while I felt fit, it had no decreasing effect on my high blood pressure. After much thought and advice, I decided to work towards a new regime where I would jog an hour a day, six days a week. In the present context, this was my development-based objective. I followed a step-by-step programme and achieved my objective. However, as noted above, like most development-based objectives, once I had reached my target, I would then need to maintain it. This would mean that, long-term, I would need to devote an hour a day to maintaining this exercise regime. I was able to integrate this objective into my life, and this has helped me to maintain it. However, many people do not give thought to the long-term implications of maintaining an objective. They are prepared to rearrange their life in the short-term so that they can *achieve* their objective, but they may not be prepared to make these rearrangements permanent so that they can *maintain* their objective, once reached. Consequently, when helping your coachee select a development-based objective, discuss the long-term implications of doing so and encourage them to choose one that can be integrated into their life once achieved.

4.1.2.6. Is your coachee prepared to make sacrifices to achieve and maintain the objective?

Following on from the example I gave in the previous section of my exercise regime objective, I realised quite early on that if I decided to work towards achieving it and to maintain it once achieved, this meant making a sacrifice, in this case of time. My new regime was 40 minutes longer than my old regime, and therefore if I was to devote that time regularly, I would have to give up an activity that was taking 40 minutes. I decided to forgo 40 minutes TV watching, which was, for me, quite an easy decision. However, not all sacrifices are as easy to make, and therefore, it is important to ask your coachee (a) what sacrifice would pursuing and maintaining their objective involve, and (b) are they prepared to make it? Help them to choose an objective for which they are prepared to make the necessary sacrifice.

4.2. Agreeing problem-based goals in coaching

The main task that you have in the goal-alliance domain of problem-focused coaching (PF-C)[16] is to help your coachee set a goal with respect to each of the problems for which they are seeking help. Again, in doing this, you need to be mindful of how many sessions you have contracted for. The more sessions you have contracted for, the more problems you can deal with and the more problem-related goals you can help your coachee achieve.

As I suggested when discussing objectives in DF-C, in PF-C, you and your coachee need to think about such questions as the following:

- How many sessions you are going to have with one another?
- How many problem-based goals has your coachee set?
- In which order does your coachee wish to deal with their problems?
- How many sessions are you going to devote to each problem/goal? This may be difficult to judge, but a rough estimate is useful.
- Is there a link between the different goals so that learning derived from pursuing one goal may be transferred to the pursuit of the other goal(s)? This may be apparent at the outset, or it will only be clear once coaching on the pursuit of goals is underway.

4.2.1. The nature of problem-based goals

As I discussed in Chapter 1, when your coachee has a problem for which they are seeking coaching, this may be because (a) they are confused, tangled up with an issue or issues and need clarity and order which they hope to get by talking things through with someone, but they are not emotionally disturbed about the issue(s) (I call this a practical problem), or (b) they have an emotionally disturbed response to an adversity, and their behaviour is unconstructive (I call this an emotional problem).

Here are two examples. The first is an example of a practical problem. One of my coachees, Ken, was struggling with a lot of work and was having difficulty prioritising. He was feeling lost and caught up in his own thoughts, but he was not unduly disturbed about things. I helped him by bringing some order to his thinking and by encouraging him to keep track of his work with reference to a written weekly activity schedule of his work activities. This helped him to regain the sense of control he felt he was losing and to prioritise his workload and focus on his tasks.

The second is an example of an emotional problem. One of my coachees, Kate, came to problem-focused coaching for help with a problem of avoidance of meetings at work which was badly affecting her career prospects. On assessment, we found that her adversity was the possibility of saying something stupid at work meetings, her unhealthy negative emotion was anxiety and her unconstructive behaviour was avoidance. I then asked Kate what she wanted to achieve. She replied that she wanted to be able to attend meetings rather than avoid them. She wanted to change her behavioural response to the meetings. The difficulty with this goal is that if she does so, she will experience anxiety, since her avoidance of meetings protects her from feeling anxious. I explained that while attending meetings was a useful goal, avoiding them was designed to protect her from feeling anxious. Then, I asked her if she was going to attend those meetings, what would her goal be with respect to her feelings of anxiety? She replied that she did not want to feel anxious at all. This is a common response, but a problematic one, since it sets the absence of a problematic emotional response as a goal, and people need to feel something under these conditions. I explained this, and Kate retorted that, in that case, she wanted to feel less anxious. This is also problematic since as anxiety is an unhealthy response to set a less intense version of an unhealthy emotion as a goal is still signing up to the problem. In the end, we agreed to set "un-anxious concern" as an emotional goal. This emotion was negative in tone, but healthy in effect, and was about the adversity that was central to her problem. This example shows that in emotional problem-focused coaching (EPF-C), it is important to set goals with respect to what the problem is about – the adversity and for the person to have a healthy negative emotional response together with a constructive behavioural response to the adversity. I have mentioned my approach to emotional problem-based goal-setting at length as a way for you to reflect on your approach to such goal-setting, and not because I want you to adopt my approach. Don't forget that, from a coaching alliance perspective, what matters is that you and your coachee agree on what their problem-based goal is.

Sometimes in response to your question about which goal your coachee wants to set with respect to their problem, the person responds with a development-based objective instead. In the case of Kate, she might have said that she wanted to improve her presentation skills in meetings, which is a development-based objective. The way I would have responded to Kate in this case would have been to agree with her objective, but to encourage her to see that, first, she needed to address her anxiety about the possibility of saying something stupid and that, to this end, I could help her to feel healthily concerned, rather than unhealthily anxious about this possible adversity. Once she had achieved this goal, I would have switched to a development-focused contract and worked with her objective to improve her public speaking skills. When your coachee has understood that it is difficult to work towards a development-based objective when they have a related adversity-based problem, they are usually amenable to set a problem-based goal first and, once this has been achieved, they can switch to working towards their development-based objective, free from the hampering effects of the problem that has now been effectively addressed.

4.2.1.1. Problem-based goals: achievement and maintenance

Once your coachee has achieved their goal, they still need to continue to do some work to maintain their gains. Once they feel confident that they can do this maintenance work on their own, you can then switch to targeting another of their problems and set a suitable goal with respect to this new target problem.

4.2.2. Maximising the chances that your coachee will achieve their problem-based goals

In the previous section, I dealt with a number of factors that would increase the chances that your coachee would achieve their development-based objectives, and I refer you to that discussion. A number of those factors are also relevant when helping your coachee to achieve their goals, and they are listed in the sections that follow.

4.2.2.1. Goal clarity

Again, some coaching approaches argue that the clearer your coachee can be about what they want to achieve with respect to their problem, the more likely they are to achieve it and/or to maintain it once achieved. Others argue that a more general "felt-sense" approach is more appropriate. Coaching alliance theory argues again that what matters is that you and your coachee agree on the level of specificity to be aimed for.

4.2.2.2. Whose problem-based goal is it?

Problem-focused coaching is likely to be more effective if the problem-based goal that your coachee has set is truly what they want to achieve. I call this goal "intrinsic goal". Sometimes it happens that a stakeholder (often an employer) refers someone for coaching because they want the person to tackle a problem that the stakeholder thinks the person has and to achieve something related to this problem. A common example is with anger where the employer has referred to person to coaching for "anger management". I call this goal an "extrinsic goal". When the person shares the employer's goal, that is when there is concordance between the intrinsic goal and the extrinsic goal, this bodes well for a good outcome since the employer can support the coachee's work towards their shared goal. However, when the coachee does not agree with their employer, but feels compelled to attend coaching, then there is a potential threat to the coaching alliance that you need to deal with. Earlier I considered the options that you face when your coachee and stakeholder do not agree on the coachee's objective (see pp. 34–36), and I refer you to that discussion as the issues are the same for disagreement on goals as they are for disagreement on objectives.

Whatever the outcome of such discussions, please remember again that from a coaching alliance perspective, effective coaching occurs when you and your coachee agree on the coachee's intrinsic goal that they have initiated.

4.2.2.3. The presence or absence of social support

As is the case with development-based objectives, when your coachee is pursuing a problem-based goal, social support can be useful to the person if they want it. So, find out from your coachee if having a social support system would encourage them to pursue their goal, and if so, help them to specify who would be in this system and suggest they ask these people if they would show their support to your coachee during PF-C.

4.2.2.4. Is your coachee prepared to make sacrifices to achieve and maintain the goal?

Before you and your coachee agree a problem-based goal, it is important that you determine whether or not your coachee is prepared to make the necessary sacrifices to achieve the goal in the first place and to maintain it in the second. In emotional problem-focused coaching (EPF-C), achieving such goals usually mean facing the adversity a number of times in order to practise whatever they have from you in coaching. This can be time-consuming and in the short and medium term, it can be uncomfortable. In my experiences, coachees who, after discussion, are willing to make time-related and comfort-related sacrifices get more out of EPF-C than coachees who are not consulted on the issue by their coaches and thus may not be prepared to make such sacrifices.

Both development-based objectives and problem-based goals are aspirational. To achieve them, your coachee needs to implement various objective-/goal-directed tasks, and you have tasks to carry out to help them to do this. I will discuss the task domain of the coaching alliance in the following and final chapter.

5 Tasks in coaching

The fourth and final domain of the coaching alliance that I wish to discuss in this book is tasks – activities carried out by you and your coachees which are objective directed in nature in development-focused coaching (DF-C) and goal directed in problem-focused coaching (PF-C). Tasks in coaching will be suggested by the approach to coaching that you take, but if you hold a pluralistic view on coaching, you can also use a variety of tasks that derive from other approaches to coaching. When you take an alliance perspective on tasks, you need to do the following:

1 *Help your coachee understand that they have coaching tasks to perform and that they know the nature of these tasks.*

If your coachee does not either explicitly or implicitly understand (a) that they have tasks to perform in the coaching process and (b) what these tasks are, then an obstacle to their progress through the coaching process exists. As with other obstacles, this may be dealt with by referring the matter for discussion to that part of the coaching dialogue that I have called 'the reflection process' where you and your coachee step back and discuss what has gone on between the two of you during coaching sessions.

2 *Help your coachee see that performing their tasks will help them to achieve their obstacles/goals.*

As I have stated, from a coaching alliance perspective, tasks are best conceptualised as ways of achieving development-based objectives in DF-C and problem-based goals in PF-C. Thus, your coachee may understand what their tasks are, but they may be uncertain how carrying these out may help them to achieve their objectives/goals. For example, your coachee may not see how questioning their distorted thinking about performance in emotional problem-focused cognitive-behavioural coaching will necessarily help them to be productively aroused rather than anxious when giving a PowerPoint presentation at work. Thus, from an alliance perspective, it is very important that you help your clients to understand the link between carrying out their coaching tasks and achieving their obstacles/goals. This holds true whether the coachee's tasks are to be performed within the coaching session or between coaching sessions in their everyday life.

3   *Help your coachee understand that they need to work to change.*

If your coachee comes to coaching thinking that you, as coach, will do all the work and all they have to do is listen and somehow they will achieve their obstacle/goal, then they will be disappointed. In practice, for coaching to be effective, your coachee needs to be an active participant in the process and has to engage in some "work". What this work consists of depends on whether you have a development-based coaching contract with your coachee or a problem-based coaching contract. Furthermore, it also depends on the nature of the tasks that your approach to coaching suggests for your coachee, as well as tasks that they suggest for themselves.

4   *Assess your coachee's capability to carry out the coaching tasks required of them. If they have the capability, proceed with these tasks, but if they do not have the capability, suggest that they use different tasks, ones that they are capable of executing.*

To engage in coaching tasks, your coachee needs to be able to perform these tasks, and it is your task to assess whether or not your coachee has this capability. Not having the capability to engage in certain coaching tasks means that no amount of training to use these tasks will help. This is in sharp contrast to the situation where your coachee may have the capability, but not the necessary *skills* to perform these tasks, in which case they will benefit from some training and/or instructions concerning the necessary skills and how to use them.

Sometimes, it is relatively easy to determine that a coachee does not have the capability to engage in certain coaching tasks. Thus, a task may require a relatively high level of intellectual intelligence, and it is clear to you that your coachee just does not have this. However, in the majority of cases, it is less clear whether or not coachee has the required capability. In such cases, the best way of determining this is trial and error. If, after a reasonable number of attempts to encourage a coachee to use a particular task and after appropriate training in task-relevant skills, the coachee still cannot engage in the task, then it is reasonable to conclude that they do not have the necessary task-related capability. Skilled coaches are able to determine this without demoralising their coachees because they have primed their coachees to see that one of their tasks as coaches is to identify appropriate tasks for their coachees, a procedure which involves trial and error. Skilled coaches also help their coachees to recognise that they bring to coaching different capabilities, and that effective coaching involves matching coaching tasks to particular coachee capabilities.

5   *Assess whether or not your coachee has the necessary skills to carry out the coaching tasks required of them, and if they do not have the skills, then train them in these skills.*

As I mentioned before, skills are different from capabilities in that your coachee may be capable of engaging in a particular coaching task, but may not know how to do this. Once your coachee is taught how to do this, then they are able to put their capability into practice. So, although the execution of particular tasks may help your coachees to achieve their objectives/goals, if they do not have the necessary skills in their repertoire to carry these out, then this poses a threat to the coaching alliance in the task domain.

From a coaching alliance perspective, if you have developed a good bond with your coachee, you are probably the best person to teach your coachee the necessary skills. If you are not the best person to teach these skills to your coachee, refer them to someone who can, and then resume coaching when this skills training has been done.

6   *Help your coachee to develop the confidence to execute the relevant tasks.*

A similar point can be made here as has been made above. Certain coachee tasks (and in particular, those that the coachee needs to carry out between sessions – the so-called homework assignments) require a certain degree of task confidence on the part of your coachee if they are to execute them successfully. So, your coachee may understand the nature of the task, see its relevance, have the ability and the skills to carry it out, but may still not do so because they predict that they don't have the confidence to do so. If this is the case, then you can prepare your coachee in one of three ways. First, you may need to help your coachee practise the task in the coaching session until they feel confident to do the tasks on their own. Second, you might encourage them to join a relevant group or organisation that specialises in teaching the skill where they can learn and practise it until they gain confidence. For example, when my coachees want to improve their public speaking skills, I suggest that they join their local group of Toastmasters (an international organisation with local chapters that helps people to deal with their fear of public speaking by giving talks in a supportive environment). Finally, you might encourage your coachee to carry out the task unconfidently, pointing out that confidence comes from the result of undertaking an activity and is rarely experienced before the activity is first attempted. It is helpful to use an analogy (e.g. driving) to help your coachee understand this important point.

7   *Ensure that the task has sufficient potency to facilitate obstacle/goal achievement.*

If all the aforementioned conditions are met (that is, your coachee understands the nature and relevance of task execution, and they have sufficient ability, skills and confidence to perform the relevant tasks), your coachee may still not gain benefit from undertaking the task because the task it may not have sufficient potency to help them achieve their development-based objective or problem-based goal. For example, certain coachee tasks, if sufficiently well carried out, will probably lead to the coachee achieving their problem-based goal. Thus, it has long been established (Rachman & Wilson, 1980) that facing up to a threatening adversity in reality, or through imagination, will help coachee in EPF-C with their anxiety problem. However, certain tasks may have much less potency to achieve a similar result. For example, it has yet to be demonstrated that examining one's distorted thinking in the coaching session rather than in the feared situation yields very much benefit in dealing with anxiety. Here, then, your task as coach is to become au fait with the current research literature on the subject at hand and not encourage your coachee to carry out a task which is unlikely, even under the most favourable conditions, to produce much benefit.

Adopting a pluralistic position is important here. Asking your coachee to suggest tasks that they think may be helpful to them in the pursuit of their development-based objective or problem-based goal is a central tenet of pluralism. Even if your coachee suggests a task that the research literature has shown to be unhelpful, this is *not* a reason not to use it in coaching, although it is perfectly in order for you to inform your coachee of the lack of evidence for their suggested task. Don't forget that research can only point to broad effects. It cannot say that a particular coaching task that is broadly ineffective will not be effective, if implemented, by a particular coachee who thinks that it may be helpful to them to execute the task. The placebo effect can be quite powerful in such instances (Tice, 1997). From a coaching alliance perspective, suggest that your coachee implements such a task and refer the matter to the reflection process after a reasonable period has passed to evaluate its effects. If, as a consequence of your coachee's experience, it transpires that the task has not been helpful, then your coachee will be open to try a different task. This "personal scientist" approach sits very well with coaching alliance theory.

8   *Refrain from using tasks or suggesting that your coachee uses those that may perpetuate their problems.*

It is important to bear in mind that what you do in problem-focused coaching, and what your coachee does both in PF-C sessions and outside coaching sessions, may serve unwittingly to perpetuate their problems rather than help them deal effectively with these problems. Thus, your coachee may, at their own behest, do various things which, while being designed to help them overcome their problems, actually have the opposite effect. For example, if your coachee has an anxiety problem, they may seek to avoid anxiety-provoking situations before they get anxious, or withdraw from these situations once they get anxious, in an attempt deal with these anxious feelings. Such behaviour prevents your coachee from facing their fears and dealing appropriately with them, and thus they remain anxious in the long run. It is important that you help your coachee to see the both the short-term and long-term effects of such strategies and to understand that dealing effectively with such problems involves being prepared to experience short-term discomfort in order to be free of the problem in the longer term.

Some coaches respond to their coachees' anxieties with inappropriate reassurance and suggestions that their coachees distract themselves when they feel anxious. In the first case, reassurance is often ineffective because when coachees are anxious, they are often not reassurable. In the second case, distraction is a form of withdrawal and, as a result, coachees again do what they need to do – face adversity armed with appropriate problem-addressing and problem-solving strategies.

9   *Help your coachee understand the nature of your tasks as coach and how these relate to their tasks and to their development-based objectives and/or problem-based goals.*

So far, I have focused on issues which deal with your coachee's tasks. However, in addition to the foregoing, it is important that your coachee understands your coaching interventions and their rationale. In particular, the more your coachee can understand how their tasks relate to your tasks as coach, the more each of you can concentrate on effective task execution, the purpose of which, as has been stressed above, is to facilitate the attainment of your coachee's development-based objectives and/or problem-based goals. Should your coachee be confused or puzzled about your tasks and how these relate to their own, they will be side-tracked from performing their own tasks and begin to question what you are doing and perhaps even your competence as a coach. These doubts, if not explored and dealt with in the reflection process, constitute a threat at all levels of the coaching alliance. An additional strategy that may prevent the development of your coachee's doubts is for you as coach to explain, at an appropriate stage, coaching, your tasks and why you are intervening in the way you have chosen to or plan to. You will maximise the impact of such explanations if you can show your coachee how your tasks complement their tasks and how both sets of tasks relate to the attainment of your coachee's development-based objectives and/or problem-based goals.

10   Ensure that your coachee is in a sufficiently good frame of mind to execute their tasks.

So far, I have outlined some of the favourable conditions that need to exist in coaching for your coachee to get the most out of coaching in the task domain. No matter how favourable these conditions are, your coachee needs to be in a sufficiently good frame of mind to capitalise on them. Thus, if one of your coachees is anxious about something in her life, then she will probably not be able to implement tasks that involve a lot of focused attention in DF-C, for example. Similarly, if another of your coachees is depressed, then he may not be able to engage in the very active coaching tasks that DF-C often involves. In such cases, it is important that you do not ask coachees to engage in coaching tasks that are too much for them at that point in time, and instead, you need to help them to deal with the issue with which they are currently preoccupied. If you don't have the skills to do so, then refer the person to a colleague who can help them, on the understanding that they will be re-referred to you for the resumption of development-based coaching when their issue has been dealt with. Asking coachees to engage in tasks that are too much for them only results in their discouragement about the coaching process. So, continually monitor your clients' frame of mind and encourage them to engage in tasks that are "challenging but not overwhelming" for them at any given point in time (Dryden, 1985).[17]

5.1. Tasks and your expertise as a coach

Your effectiveness as a coach is partly dependent on your expertise as a practitioner. I say partly here, because no matter how expert you are in carrying out your coaching tasks, unless your coachee carries out their tasks, then coaching will not be effective. Here is a sample of issues that pertain to your expertise in executing your tasks.

5.1.1. Coach skill

From a coaching alliance perspective, the degree to which your coachee makes progress may be due in some measure to the skill with which you perform your tasks as coach. If you are skilful in the execution of your tasks, you increase the chances that your clients will have confidence in your ability and see you as being helpful (Pinsof & Catherall, 1986). However, it is important that you realise that you develop skill as a coach gradually and that if you want to be competent as a coaching practitioner, you need to accept moving from a state of conscious incompetence to conscious competence and hence to unconscious competence.

5.1.2. Making judicious referrals

It is important to realise that not everyone who seeks coaching from you will be suitable for that help. This may be the case for a number of reasons. First, they may be looking for a different type of help. For example, some people come for coaching for advice on how to change others and are not interested in looking at their own contribution to their relationships. Second, the person applying for your help may be suitable for coaching, but may want a very different approach to coaching than you can offer. Third, the person may be seeking coaching, may be suitable for the approach to coaching that you practise, but you consider that you may not be the best person to see them. Thus, the person may be better helped by a coach of the same gender as themselves, but different from yours, or they may be better helped by someone who has a different personality type than you. Furthermore, your coachee may be seeking coaching which requires specialist knowledge or skills that you don't possess, but you know a colleague who does possess that knowledge or those skills.

It follows from the above that determining the best type of help for the people who have come to see you and making a judicious referral if necessary are core skills that you need to develop as a coach. It is particularly important when you make a referral that you inspire the person with the hope that the coach to whom you are referring them is the best person that you know who can offer the most appropriate help.

5.1.3. Varying your use of coaching tasks

A theme that has run through this book, albeit implicitly, is that since coachees differ (along several key dimensions), coaches need to vary their own contribution to the coaching process. This has clear implications for coachee objectives and/or goals since there is more than one way to help your coachee, and if one set of coach tasks is not helpful to particular coachees then others may be.

My late friend and colleague Dr Arnold Lazarus (1989) argued that there are seven modalities of human experience that need to be considered when working with coachees: Behaviour, Affect (or Emotions), Sensation, Imagery, Cognition (or Thinking), Interpersonal Relationships and Physiological Functioning. These seven modalities are known by the acronym BASIC ID (the D stands for drugs, the most common way of dealing with problems in the physiological functioning modality). Lazarus argued that people vary according to the modalities that they typically use and that it is useful to develop a person's modality profile by asking them to rate themselves on a 0–10 scale indicating varying degree of modality use.

Let me show how this informed my work with two coachees experiencing a similar anger problem for which they sought emotional problem-focused coaching (EPF-C). Clive scored highly on the behavioural, interpersonal and sensation modalities. I helped Clive use these modalities particularly when he first noticed himself getting angry by encouraging him to use a sensory (in this case, olfactory) cue to relax (the smell of his girlfriend's perfume), before capitalising on his strong tendency to use the behavioural and interpersonal modalities. Here, I encouraged him to use his assertive skills with the person with whom he was angry. Stephen, on the other hand, scored high on the cognitive and imagery modalities, but low on the behavioural and interpersonal modalities. Therefore, I taught Stephen cognitive restructuring techniques to deal with provocations before encouraging him to see himself, in his mind's eye, asserting himself with the person with whom he was angry. I then encouraged him to use assertion in real life. Since, in general, people require more help in using tasks in their non-preferred modalities, I spent more time in coaching on teaching Stephen how to assert himself in real life than I did with Clive.

From the above, it is clear that it is useful to know your coachee's modality strengths in developing a jointly negotiated coaching plan. But sometimes, you will need to help your coachee to become more proficient in the modalities in which they are less proficient. For example, a very passive coachee often needs to learn to be more active in the behavioural modality.

Extrapolating from Lazarus's (1989) work, it is important to note that coaches also have preferred modalities. While in an ideal world, effective coaches would, with equal facility, be able to use tasks across the BASIC ID, the fact that coaches have their own modality preferences means that it is a temptation for them to restrict themselves to using tasks which reflect these preferences. If coaches restrict themselves to using particular intervention modalities (e.g. cognitive, emotive or behavioural), they would help a smaller range of coachees than if they became more flexible in freely and appropriately using tasks across the BASIC ID. It follows from this that to increase your effectiveness in the task domain of the alliance, you need to acknowledge your own task preferences and work on broadening your range of task behaviour – a task which itself calls for continual exposure to what coaching models other than your own preferred model have to offer. This is a feature of a pluralistic approach to coaching which is a theme of this book. If coaches do not accept the challenge of broadening their task-related repertoire, then what they need to do, as discussed above, is to refer coachees who are likely to benefit from different coaching approaches to practitioners of these approaches. To assume that one's own approach will help everyone is a misguided 'one-size-fits-all' viewpoint that open-minded practitioners tend not to hold.

5.1.4. *Capitalising on the client's learning style*

As used here, coaching tasks (broadly conceptualised) are the means by which coachees achieve their development-based objectives and/or problem-based goals. If coachees do achieve their objectives/goals, it is because they have learned something new (for example, to see things differently and/or to act differently).

Taking a coaching alliance perspective on client learning, you need to consider how best to facilitate learning for each of your coachees. For example, you need to discover how each of your coachees learns best and capitalise on this by tailoring your interventions accordingly.

Let me illustrate this by discussing two coachees who came to see me for emotional problem-focused coaching (EPF-C) and who had similar problems, but different learning styles. Susan and Leona both experienced anxiety about public speaking and avoided it whenever they could. They were both worried that they would say something foolish while speaking formally in public. They were both referred for coaching because neither would accept a referral for counselling or psychotherapy. Susan learned best by finding out how other people had overcome similar fears and applying what made sense to her from their experiences. Leona, on the other hand, said that it was important to her to discover the possible origins of her fear before learning how to deal with it.

I encouraged Susan to surf the net and develop a portfolio of how others had successfully dealt with this fear. I also suggested that she attend Toastmasters, an organisation that helps people give public speeches where she met people who had a problem with public speaking and who had learned how to speak in public without anxiety. As a result of these experiences, I encouraged Susan to put together a way of tackling the problem that was right for her.

With Leona, I took a very different tack. I helped her to review her past experiences of speaking in public, and she discovered that her problem started after her teacher had joked about how squeaky her voice sounded when he had heard her speak in a school play when she was ten years of age. I helped her to understand the dysfunctional attitudes she had formed as a result of this experience and was still unwittingly perpetuating by avoiding public speaking. For Leona, practising healthy alternatives to these dysfunctional attitudes while revisiting in imagination that early experience was an important precursor to practising those new attitudes in the present. By contrast, I never discussed the possible historical roots of Susan's problem because she did not mention this as an important ingredient of her learning style.

5.1.5. *Helping your coachee to get the most out of their coaching tasks*

Given the fact that your coachee has tasks to carry out in coaching, however specifically or broadly these tasks are conceived, what should you do to help your coachee get the most out of these tasks? Here is a selection of possible interventions:

1   Negotiate with your coachee what their tasks are.
2   Help your coachee see clearly the relationship between their tasks and their coaching objectives and/or goals. Encourage them to keep this connection clearly in mind during coaching.

3   Modify these tasks after taking into account your coachee's strengths and weaknesses. You can do this before your coachee carries out their tasks and after they have done so. In the latter case, you can modify the tasks based on your coachee's feedback on their attempts to use them.

4   Train your coachee in these tasks if relevant.

5   Problem solve any obstacles to coachee task execution.

6   Have alternative coachee tasks in mind if your coachee does not want to or cannot carry out their original tasks.

7   If you negotiate homework assignments with your coachee, make sure that they specify what they are going to do, when they are going to do it and how often. Problem solve possible obstacles to homework completion.

5.1.6. Using different tasks in the two different types of coaching

I have made a distinction between two different types of coaching: problem-focused coaching (PF-C), where your coachee comes to see you because they have a problem (or problems) for which they seek help, and development-focused coaching (DF-C), where your coachee comes to see you because they wish to get more out of themselves, their career and/or their personal life. These different types of coaching do require different tasks. Broadly speaking, in DF-C, your tasks, and that of your coachee, are focused on the promotion of the coachee's development and growth. In practical problem-focused coaching (PPF-C), your respective tasks are mainly to help your coachee gain greater clarity on the issues that they are facing so that they can problem solve more effectively. While in emotional problem-focused coaching (EPF-C), your respective tasks are focused on helping your coachee deal healthily with adversity. Difficulties occur in coaching where coaches use and suggest that coachees use tasks that are not appropriate for the type of coaching they have both contracted for, but are more appropriate for the other type of coaching. The issue for coaches who are primarily counsellors and therapists is that they tend to be more comfortable working with problems, and thus, there is a tendency to want to practice EPF-C. The issue for coaches who are primarily trained as coaches is that they tend to flounder when faced with coachees' emotional problems. This is why the compleat coach is equally at home in both types of coaching and can move with ease from the one type to the other.

5.1.7. *Using tasks at different stages of coaching*

It is likely that your tasks as coach and your coachee's tasks will change during the coaching process. From a coaching alliance perspective, it is important that you both understand this and feel able to refer the matter to the reflection process if you need to discuss it.

5.1.7.1. *How your coaching tasks change over time*

The main change in your coaching tasks over time is that at the beginning of coaching, you will be probably quite active in the process. As coaching progresses, your level of activity will decrease as you will encourage your coachee to take greater responsibility for their coaching and carry out some of the tasks that you initiated earlier in the process, so that towards the end, you will become more of a consultant than a coach. This means that you will prompt your coachee when they falter at self-coaching rather than take more of an active interventionist role.

In what follows, I list your coaching tasks roughly in the order that you will carry them out to give you a sense of how your tasks vary over time.

During coaching, you will do such things as the following:

- Determine whether the person seeking help is a good candidate for coaching and, if so, which type of coaching is most appropriate.
- Negotiate consent with your coachee.
- Introduce the concept of the reflection process and explain how it works.
- Help your coachee to set development-based objectives or problem-based goals.
- Discuss with your coachee which tasks they are able and willing to do in order to achieve their objective and/or goal.
- Help your coachee to plan to carry out their tasks.
- Encourage them to initiate and maintain the plan.
- Train your coachee to use skills that they are capable of using, but are not in their skills repertoire.
- Discuss how their plan needs to be altered based on their experiences of task execution.
- Help your coachee to anticipate potential obstacles and intervene so that they don't become actual obstacles.
- Help your coachee to identify and deal with any actual obstacles that do occur.

- Once your coachee has achieved their objectives and/or goals, help them to maintain and enhance their gains within the specified life area or problem to other life areas or problems.
- Develop an agreed plan with your coachee to end coaching.
- Set up agreed follow-up sessions.

5.1.7.2. How your coachee's tasks change over time

Your coachee's tasks also change over time, and while effective coaching is characterised by your coachee's active involvement in the process, as pointed out before, as coaching unfolds, you will become more of a consultant to the change process, and they will assume increasingly greater responsibility for managing their own change.

In what follows, I list your coachee's tasks again roughly in the order that they will carry them out to give you a sense of how their tasks vary over time.

During coaching, your coachee will be expected to do such things as the following:

- Inform you of where they are in their life and where they would like to be in DF-C (i.e. set objectives), and what their problems are and what help they are looking for with respect to these problems in PF-C (i.e. set goals)
- Give consent to proceed after a period of negotiation
- Give honest reactions to your suggestions about how you would approach coaching with them and on other matters in the reflection process
- Give their suggestions about what would be helpful to them in coaching
- Engage with you in developing an action plan with respect to their objectives and/or goals
- Initiate and maintain the tasks specified in the action plan and be prepared to modify the plan in response to their experiences of carrying out agreed tasks
- Predict and deal with potential obstacles
- Disclose and deal with actual obstacles
- Work out a plan with you to maintain and enhance gains
- Work out a plan to end coaching
- Engage in agreed follow-up sessions

This brings us to the end of this book. I hope you have found the discussion of the coaching alliance helpful to you and that it will encourage you to consider each of the domains of the alliance as you continue your career as a coach. In the spirit of coaching, I invite feedback that might help improve future editions of this book. Please email me at windy@windydryden.com.

Notes

1 I prefer the term *negotiated consent* to the more traditional *informed consent*. In the latter, coachees are passive. They are informed by the coach, and then they either give their consent, or not. In the former, coachees are active. They are informed by the coach, but they also inform the coach about their preferences and give their consent, or not, after a period of negotiation. I will discuss this in Chapter 3.

2 See above.

3 Some problems may have practical and emotional components. This issue lies outside of the scope of this book.

4 Currently often referred to as *respect*.

5 I prefer the term *acceptance* to *unconditional positive regard* or *respect*.

6 George Kelly was the originator of personal construct psychology.

7 In this section, please assume that whenever I say that PF-C may not be indicated, I suggest that the coach refers the person to a suitable mental health specialist.

8 CBT Oxford, Cognitive behavioral coaching, www.cbtoxford.com/cbt-coaching-oxford-companies-groups as of 22/12/16.

9 Gladeana McMahon, Personal coaching services, *Cognitive Behavioural Coaching Works!*, www.cognitivebehaviouralcoachingworks.com/individual-coaching-services/ as of 22/12/16.

10 By "your specific approach", I don't just mean what school of coaching you are most closely associated, but what distinguishes your approach. This may be an eclectic, integrative or pluralistic approach. Whatever it is, you need to explain this to your coachee.

11 See Cavanagh's (2005) criteria discussed earlier in this chapter.

12 See the discussion on obstacles below.

13 In this book, when I use the term *obstacle*, I mean actual obstacle.

14 For all intents and purposes, a problem and obstacle can be treated the same as both involve the presence of an adversity and a disturbed response to this adversity which leads the person to become stuck.

15 Please remember that in this book, I use the term *objectives* to reflect the aims of DF-C and the term *goals* to reflect the aims of PF-C. I also use the term goals

to refer to what the person wants to achieve in addressing the obstacles to the pursuit of their development-based objectives or problem-based goals.

16 When discussing goals in this section, I refer to goals with respect to problems in PF-C, as noted, and goals with respect to actual obstacles in DF-C.

17 Conversely, asking coachees to engage in tasks that are insufficiently challenging for them may also deprive them of the opportunity of getting the most out of coaching.

References

Bannister, D., & Fransella, F. (1986). *Inquiring man: The psychology of personal constructs*. London: Croom-Helm.

Bordin, E.S. (1979). The generalizability of the psychoanalytic concept of the working alliance. *Psychotherapy: Theory, Research and Practice, 16*, 252–260.

Cavanagh, M.J. (2005). Mental-health issues and challenging clients in executive coaching. In M.J. Cavanagh, A.M. Grant, & T. Kemp (Eds.), *Evidence-based coaching: Theory, research and practice from the behavioural sciences* (pp. 21–36). Bowen Hills, QLD: Australian Academic Press.

Clutterbuck, D. (2010). Welcome to the world of virtual coaching and mentoring. In D. Clutterbuck & Z. Hussain (Eds.), *Virtual coach, virtual mentor*. Charlotte, NC: Information Age Publishing Inc.

Cooper, M., & McLeod, J. (2011). *Pluralistic counselling and psychotherapy*. London: Sage.

Dorn, F.J. (Ed.). (1984). *The social influence process in counseling and psychotherapy*. Springfield, IL: Charles C. Thomas.

Downey, M. (2014). *Effective modern coaching: The principles and art of successful business coaching*. London: LID Publishing.

Dryden, W. (1997). Dilemmas in giving love or warmth to clients: An interview with Albert Ellis. In W. Dryden (Ed.), *Therapists' dilemmas* (2nd ed., pp. 5–16). London: Sage.

Dryden, W. (2000). *Overcoming anxiety*. London: Sheldon.

Dryden, W. (2003). *Letting go of anxiety and depression*. London: Sheldon.

Dryden, W. (2006). *Counselling in a nutshell*. London: Sage.

Dryden, W. (2011a). *Counselling in a nutshell* (2nd ed.). London: Sage.

Dryden, W. (2011b). *Manage your anxiety through CBT*. London: Hodder Education.

Dryden, W. (2012). The therapeutic relationship in CBT. In W. Dryden & R. Branch (Eds.), *The CBT handbook* (pp. 83–100). London: Sage.

Dryden, W. (2017). *Very brief cognitive-behavioural coaching*. Abingdon, Oxon: Routledge.

Dryden, W. (2018). *Cognitive-emotive-behavioural coaching: A flexible and pluralistic approach*. Abingdon, Oxon: Routledge.

Garvin, C.D., & Seabury, B.A. (1997). *Interpersonal practice in social work:* Promoting *competence and social justice* (2nd ed.). Boston, MA: Allyn & Bacon.

Gessnitzer, S., & Kauffeld, S. (2015). The working alliance in coaching: Why behaviour is the key to success. *The Journal of Applied Behavioral Science, 51,* 177–197.

Grant, A.M., & Cavanagh, M.J. (2010). Life coaching. In E. Cox, T. Bachkirova, & D. Clutterbuck (Eds.), *The complete handbook of coaching* (pp. 297–310). London: Sage.

Gyllensten, K., & Palmer, S. (2007). The coaching relationship: An interpretative phenomenological analysis. *International Coaching Psychology Review, 2*(2), 168–176.

Ianiro, P.M., Lehmann-Willenbrock, N., & Kauffeld, S. (2015). Coaches and clients in action: A sequential analysis of interpersonal coach and client behaviour. *Journal of Business Psychology, 3,* 435–456.

Iordanou, I., Hawley, R., & Iordanou, C. (2017). *Values and ethics in coaching.* London: Sage Publications.

Katsikis, D., Kostogiannis, C., & Dryden, W. (2016). A rational-emotive behavior approach in life coaching. *Journal of Evidence-Based Psychotherapies, 16*(1), 3–18.

Lazarus, A.A. (1989). *The practice of multi-modal therapy: Systematic, comprehensive and effective psychotherapy.* Baltimore, MD: The Johns Hopkins University Press.

Lazarus, A.A. (1993). Tailoring the therapeutic relationship, or being an authentic chameleon. *Psychotherapy: Theory, Research & Practice, 30,* 404–407.

Machin, S. (2010). The nature of the internal coaching relationship. *International Journal of Evidence Based Coaching and Mentoring, 4,* 37–52.

Maslow, A. (1968). *Toward a psychology of being* (2nd ed.). New York: Van Nostrand Reinhold.

O'Broin, A., & Palmer, S. (2009). Co-creating an optimal coaching alliance: A cognitive behavioural coaching perspective. *International Coaching Psychology Review, 4,* 184–194.

O'Broin, A., & Palmer, S. (2010a). The coaching alliance as a universal concept spanning conceptual approaches. *Coaching Psychology International, 3*(1), 3–6.

O'Broin, A., & Palmer, S. (2010b). Exploring key aspects in the formation of coaching relationships: Initial indicators from the perspective of the coachee and the coach. *Coaching: An International Journal of Theory, Research and Practice, 3,* 124–143.

Palmer, S. (2008). The PRACTICE model of coaching: Towards a solution-focused approach. *Coaching Psychology International, 1*(1), 4–6.

Pinsof, W.M., & Catherall, D. (1986). The integrative psychotherapy alliance: Family, couple, individual therapy scales. *Journal of Marital and Family Therapy, 12,* 137–151.

Rachman, S.J., & Wilson, G.T. (1980). *The effects of psychological therapy* (2nd enlarged ed.). New York: Pergamon.

Rogers, C.R. (1957). The necessary and sufficient conditions of therapeutic personality change. *Journal of Consulting Psychology, 21*, 95–103.

Tice, L., & Quick, J. (1997). *Personal coaching for results*. Nashville, TN: Thomas Nelson.

Index